Breathe In, Breathe Out

Practicing Movement

Reach Out!

Learning to overcome negative thoughts and stay mindful is not the same as fighting depression. Do you feel overwhelmed by sadness? Remember, you matter. You are not alone. If you need help, reach out. Talk to an adult you love and trust. This could be a teacher, school counselor, or family member. Make an appointment with your doctor. Seek professional help. Or call the National Suicide Prevention Lifeline at 1-800-273-8255. Someone is available to talk with you 24 hours a day, every day.

Published in the United States of America by Cherry Lake Publishing
Ann Arbor, Michigan
www.cherrylakepublishing.com

Reading Adviser: Marla Conn, MS, Ed., Literacy specialist, Read-Ability, Inc.
Book Designer: Melinda Millward

Photo Credits: © mirzamlk/Shutterstock.com, back cover, 8; © Deepak Sethi/istockphoto.com, cover, 5; © kuroksta/Shutterstock.com, 6, 14, 18; © mentatdgt/Shutterstock.com, 7; © Sho Oda/Shutterstock.com, 9; © Rob Marmion/Shutterstock.com, 9; © MAKSIM ANKUDA/Shutterstock.com, 10, 22; © mixetto/istockphoto.com, 11; © Ben Gingell/Shutterstock.com, 12; © MaKo-studio/Shutterstock.com,15; © Emeraldora/Shutterstock.com, 16; © SolStock/istockphoto.com, 17; © dmbaker/istockphoto.com, 19; © Hogan Imaging/Shutterstock.com, 20; © Merla/Shutterstock.com, 23; © Wouter Tolenaars/Shutterstock.com, 24; © popicon/Shutterstock.com, 26; © WAYHOME studio/Shutterstock.com, 27; © guas /stock.adobe.com, 28; © Lopolo/Shutterstock.com, 30;

Graphic Element Credits: © kkoman/Shutterstock.com, back cover, front cover, multiple interior pages; © str33t cat/Shutterstock.com, front cover, multiple interior pages; © NotionPic/Shutterstock.com, multiple interior pages; © CARACOLLA/Shutterstock.com, multiple interior pages; © VikiVector/Shutterstock.com, multiple interior pages

45th Parallel Press is an imprint of Cherry Lake Publishing.

Library of Congress Cataloging-in-Publication Data has been filed and is available at catalog.loc.gov

Printed in the United States of America
Corporate Graphics

Table of Contents

INTRODUCTION

Have you ever found yourself unable to sit still? Some people get nervous. They get worried. They get sad. They can't control their feelings or actions. This is why it's important to practice intentional movement. Intentional means doing something on purpose. We need to connect our minds and bodies. This will let us manage different challenges. This will help us be more aware.

We focus better when we better control our movements. We breathe on purpose. We move on purpose. We use our body to lead our mind.

This book gives you tips on how to be **mindful**. Mindful means being aware. It means taking care of your body and mind. Take a moment. Practice moving. Just breathe …

Tip: Choose to move.

CHAPTER ONE
Hold That Pose

Yoga is the practice of quieting the mind. It combines breathing techniques, exercise, and **meditation**. Meditation is deep thinking. It focuses the mind for a period of time. **Inversions** are popular yoga moves. Inversions are changes in position that bring the head below the heart. It's a calming pose.

Here are some inversion yoga poses you can try:

- Bend over. Touch your toes. Feel the stretch in your lower back. Let your head and hands hang heavy.
- Do a headstand against a wall. Or ask a friend to help.
- Kneel and sit on your heels. Sit up straight. Bring your chest to your thighs. Bring your forehead down to the floor. Stretch your arms out long. You can stretch them in front of you. Or you can stretch them behind you.

Tip: Loosen up your body. Shake out your arms. Shake out your legs.

There are other moves to help you connect your mind and body:

- Start on all fours. Pretend your back is a table. Tuck your toes under. Then press your hands on the floor and lift your hips up toward the ceiling. Straighten your legs. Make an upside-down V-shape. Press your heels toward the floor. Feel the stretch. Let your head and neck hang freely. Breathe. Hold the pose.
- Sit up on the floor with a straight spine. Place the bottoms of your feet together. Grab hold of your ankles. Gently bounce your knees toward the floor. Do this 10 to 20 times.
- Lie on your back. Stretch out your arms and legs. Raise and lower 1 arm at a time toward the ceiling. Lift and lower 1 leg at a time toward the ceiling. Try lifting your arm and the opposite leg at the same time.

Tip: Try these movements in a hot room. Prepare to sweat!

Chapter Two
Stand Tall

We spend our day either lying down, sitting, or standing. We do these things without thinking about it. The next time you stand, choose to do some mindful standing. First, stand with purpose. Second, think about your body while you stand. Think about your muscle groups.

Try some of these standing moves:

- Stand straight. Hang your arms heavy by your side. Imagine a balloon is attached to the top of your head. The balloon is gently pulling you up.
- Stand straight. Breathe in. Lift your heels up. Breathe out. Let your heels fall back down. Lift your toes up. Rock up and down. Do this for 5 breaths.

Tip: Take a walk. Think about how your feet feel inside your shoes.

After trying a few mindful standing moves, stay standing. Keep your body still. Close your eyes. Take a mindful minute. Focus on what it feels like to be in your body. Use these prompts to help you focus:

- Take a minute to listen. Listen closely to the sounds around you. Listen closely to the sounds inside you.
- Feel your heartbeat. Feel your chest and belly rising and falling.
- Think about your energy level before trying the standing moves. Think about your energy level after.
- Think about your feelings. Did your feelings change? Did they stay the same?

Tip: Take your pulse. Track your heartbeats. Do this at different times of the day.

Real-Life Scenarios

Life is full of adventures. There will be challenges. Be prepared to make good choices. These are some events you could face:

- You broke a bone. Or you strained a muscle. Your body is healing. But you still feel weak and sore. You want to get better. How can you safely move more?

- You're stressed out. Your neck and shoulders feel tight. You're getting headaches. What breathing exercises could you do? What movement exercises could you do?

- You can't focus. Your thoughts are everywhere. You are pacing. You're playing with your hands. You're tapping your feet. How can you calm your body? How can you control your body more?

Chapter Three
Go with the Flow

Tai Chi comes from China. Tai Chi is a system of **physical** exercises. Physical means of the body. Tai Chi is about the flow of the life force through the body. It's all about gentle and slow movements. Movements are focused. They're combined with deep breathing. One movement flows into another movement.

Warm-ups are done before exercising. They prepare your body for harder work. Try some of these warm-ups:

- Gently circle your head to the left. Then, circle it to the right.
- Put your hands on your hips. Bend down to your toes. Slowly, stand back up.
- Stretch out your arms. Move them in circles.

Tip: Take a self-defense class. Tai Chi was originally developed as a martial art.

Next, try these Tai Chi moves. Remember to move slowly from one movement to the next.

- Practice the "**Warrior** and **Scholar**" move. Warriors are fighters. Scholars are people who study. Place your feet side by side and facing forward. Relax your hands at your sides. Breathe in. Bend your knees to a comfortable position. Keep your left hand flat. Ball up your right hand into a fist. Place your hands together. Your left hand should cover your right fist. Slowly stand up straight again. Breathe out. Repeat this process.
- Practice the "Wave Hands in Clouds" move. Stand up straight with your feet shoulder-width apart. Bring your arms out in front of you, the left arm on the bottom and the right on top. Pretend you're hugging a large ball. Twist your waist and shift to the left. Move your hands with your body. Twist your waist again and shift to the right. Switch the position of your right and left arms as you twist. As your top arm switches position with your bottom arm, slowly turn your palm to face out. Repeat this process.

Tip: Repeat movements several times. This works muscles better.

CHAPTER FOUR
Sit Up and Move

Sitting is a **sedentary** activity. Sedentary means inactive. Too much sitting is bad for the body. It can cause aches and pains. Sitting doesn't have to be inactive. Move while sitting.

While sitting, take deep breaths. For example, do the "Breath of Fire." This is a breathing exercise in yoga. It helps release stress. It can help you feel calm. Sit with your arms up in the air. Make a fist with your hands. Take a deep breath. Breathe in through your nose. Pause for a moment. Hold your breath. As you breathe out of your mouth, pull your elbows down to your waist. Repeat this in short bursts about 20 to 30 times. Pretend you're shushing someone. Say, "Sh. Sh. Sh." Every time you breathe out, pull your belly back into your spine.

Tip: Reach arms high. Feel the stretch in your spine. Pretend like you're climbing a rope. Feel your rib cage move.

Here are some movements to do while sitting:

- Sit on the edge of a chair. Lean forward. Keep your lower back arched. Face your palms together. Lift your arms out to the side like you're flying. Pause. Slowly return to the starting position. Repeat this.
- Sit on the edge of a chair. Bend your legs with your knees at a right angle. Touch your toes to the floor. Hold the armrest with your hands. Lean back. Pull your legs to your chest. Make a V-shape. Stretch out your legs. Pull your legs back to your chest. Drop your feet without touching the floor. Repeat this.
- Sit against the chair. Keep your back straight. Bend your legs at your knees. Run in place. Run with short, quick steps. Run as fast as you can. Do this for 45 seconds.

Tip: Do jumping jacks while sitting. Move your legs and arms.

Spotlight Biography

In 2017, Tabay Atkins was 10 years old. He became the youngest certified yoga teacher. Certified means official. Tabay lives in San Clemente, California. His family owns a yoga studio. Studios are places where people can do yoga. Tabay's mother was sick. She did yoga. She got better. This inspired Tabay. He trained to be a yoga teacher. He was 6 years old when he started. When he finished 5th grade, his mother gave him a gift. She said he could go to Europe or study yoga. Tabay chose to study yoga. He completed 200 hours of yoga training. He was the youngest person to do so. He teaches at his family's yoga studio. He donates his earnings to help kids with cancer. He doesn't teach for money. He does it because he loves yoga. He said, "It's about healing the mind and body. I also like to see people progress throughout the classes."

Chapter Five
Play with Balloons

Balloons are great **props** for mindful movements. Props are things used for a purpose. Balloons are filled with air. Think of them as a life force. There are many movement exercises with balloons.

Play "Balloon Toss." Toss a balloon up in the air. Gently use your hands. Keep the balloon in the air. Focus on not letting the balloon touch the ground. Add more balloons. Move slowly. Pay attention to how you move. Instead of hands, try using your breath. Breathe in. Breathe out. Keep the balloon afloat with your breath. Try long breaths. Try short breaths.

Tip: Play with bubbles. Chase bubbles. Try to pop as many as you can.

Play “Be a Balloon.” Pretend you’re a balloon. Blow yourself up by making yourself big. Float around like you’re in the air. Then, release the air. Make yourself smaller. Move in a straight line like the air inside you is rushing out. Now, pretend you’re a balloon filled with different things, not air. Here are some ideas:

- Pretend to fill your balloon with heavy rocks.
- Pretend to fill your balloon with light feathers.

Compare the differences. Think about how you’d move. Think about how you’d change your movements.

Tip: Get a tennis ball. Grip it. Squeeze hard. Relax. Repeat 20 times. Switch hands.

Science Connection

Motor skills are muscle movements. There are 2 types. Gross motor skills are large movements. Examples are crawling, running, and jumping. They are learned first. They become automatic. Fine motor skills are small movements. They're learned over time. They're more precise and specific actions. Examples are easier actions like writing, picking up things, and smacking lips. The cerebellum controls your motor skills. The cerebellum is at the back of the brain. Its name means "little brain." It's about the size of a small fist. The cerebellum is the most complex part of the brain. It has about 40 million nerves. Nerves send information from a body part to the brain. They process and control movements. The cerebellum provides balance, precision, and timing. It's also connected to learning, language, and feelings.

Chapter Six
Pretend You're a Mirror

Mindful movement means focusing on our own bodies. It's also about being aware of our **surroundings**. Surroundings are the things around us. "Mirror Games" are a great way to practice mindful movements. Games can be played with others or by yourself. Mirror Games are quiet games. The idea is to pay careful attention.

Players have to study each other's movements. The partners face each other. One partner is the leader. The other is the follower. The leader makes movements. The follower copies exactly what the leader is doing. This is done for 5 minutes. Then, you switch roles. If possible, change partners.

Tip: Copy an animal's movement. Notice how your muscles move differently than theirs.

Don't have a partner? That's okay! There are different ways to play mirror games by yourself:

- Turn on the television. Turn off the sound. Copy an actor's movements.
- Look into a mirror. Make movements. Move in slow motion. Use all your body parts. Describe what you're doing. For example, say, "Now, I am wiggling my ears."

Reflect on this game. Answer these questions:

- Is it harder to copy slow or fast movements? Why?
- Was it easier to lead or follow? Why?
- Would you rather be the leader or follower?
- How did changing partners change your focus?
- What did you learn about others? What did you learn about yourself?

Tip: Move around your room. Find 5 things you never noticed before.

Fun Fact

There are many types of yoga. There's even goat yoga! Goat yoga is officially called *caprine vinyasa*. It's yoga with baby goats. The baby goats are called kids. Kids weigh about 15 pounds (7 kilograms). They climb on people's backs. They stay there while people do yoga moves. The idea is to balance nature and movement. The kids represent nature. Goat yoga was founded by Lainey Morse. It started in 2016. Morse owns a farm in Oregon. Her farm is called No Regrets. Morse had 8 goats. She hosted a party. She invited people to hang out with her goats. Morse's yoga teacher asked if she could do some yoga at the party. Morse said, "Okay, but the goats have to join in." Now, goat yoga is popular. Morse said, "It may sound silly. But…it's helping people cope with whatever they're going through."

HOST YOUR OWN MINDFULNESS EVENT!

Feeling tense? Feeling tired? Do you need to move your body? Do you need to loosen up? This might be the best time to host your own mindfulness event! Host a "Let's Move" Party!

STEP ONE: Figure out where you can host your party. You'll need space to move around. An open area would be best.

STEP TWO: Make invitations—and get creative! Ask a friend to help you. Send out the invitations.

STEP THREE: Lead the group movements.

Let's Squat!

- Loosen your hips and thighs. Your legs get tight from sitting too much.
- Stand straight.
- Separate your feet wider than your hips.
- Breathe in. As you do this, reach your arms over your head.
- Breathe out. As you do this, bend your knees and pull your elbows down toward your knees.
- Breathe in again. Straighten your arms and legs as you inhale.
- Repeat for 5 breaths.

Let's Do the Twist!

- Stand straight.
- Separate your feet wider than your hips.
- Swing your arms like a helicopter. Swing them from side to side. Do this slowly.
- Pick up speed if it feels good.
- Breathe in and out. Gently twist your spine with each twist.
- Repeat for 5 breaths.

Let's Go Skiing!

- Stand straight.
- Separate your feet wider than your hips.
- Bend your knees.
- Put your elbows on your knees.
- Reach your arms back.
- Breathe in. Breathe out. Reach your arms over your head. Reach back. Look up.
- Breathe out. Keep your core strong.
- Repeat for 5 breaths.

GLOSSARY

inversions (in-VUR-zhuhnz) reversals of position, to be upside down

meditation (med-ih-TAY-shuhn) a focused form of deep thinking for a period of time

mindful (MINDE-ful) focusing one's awareness on the present moment to center the mind, body, and soul

physical (FIZ-ih-kuhl) of the body

props (PRAHPS) things used for a purpose

scholar (SKAH-lur) a learned person who studies things

sedentary (SED-in-ter-ee) inactive

surroundings (suh-ROUN-dingz) things around us like buildings, nature, and people

Tai Chi (TYE CHEE) Chinese system of physical exercises that focus on the flow of the life force through the body; gentle and slow movements combine with deep breathing

warm-ups (WORM-uhps) activities done before exercising to prepare the body for hard work

warrior (WOR-ee-ur) fighter

yoga (YOH-guh) the practice of quieting the mind by combining breathing techniques, exercise, and meditation

INDEX

About the Author

Dr. Virginia Loh-Hagan is an author, university professor, and former classroom teacher. She did yoga for a hot second. The yoga teacher kicked her out for laughing. She lives in San Diego with her very tall husband and very naughty dogs. To learn more about her, visit www.virginialoh.com.